THE HISTORY OF GOSPEL MUSIC

AFRICAN-AMERICAN ACHIEVERS

THE HISTORY OF GOSPEL MUSIC

Rose Blue and Corinne J. Naden

CHELSEA HOUSE PUBLISHERS
Philadelphia

Chelsea House Publishers
Editor in Chief Sally Cheney
Associate Editor in Chief Kim Shinners
Production Manager Pamela Loos
Director of Photography Judy Hasday
Art Director Sara Davis

**Produced by Pre-Press Company, Inc.,
East Bridgewater, MA 02333**

The Chelsea House World Wide Web address is
http://www.chelseahouse.com

3 5 7 9 8 6 4 2

Library of Congress Cataloging-in-Publication Data

Blue, Rose.
The history of gospel music / Rose Blue and Corinne J. Naden.
p. cm. — (African-American achievers)
Includes bibliographical references (p.) and index.
ISBN 0-7910-5818-2 (hc: alk. paper) —
ISBN 0-7910-5819-0 (pbk.: alk. paper)
1. Gospel music—History and criticism—Juvenile literature.
[1. Gospel music—History and criticism.] I. Naden, Corinne
J. II. Title. III. Series.

ML3187.B58 2001
782.25'4'09—dc21   2001028376

Frontispiece: *Members of a Southern Baptist congregation in Memphis
sing at a Sunday service. The traditions of gospel music continue to live
and grow in churches across the
country.*

CONTENTS

AFRICAN-AMERICAN ACHIEVERS

THE HISTORY OF GOSPEL MUSIC

Prologue

What Is Gospel Music?

THE *HARPER DICTIONARY of Music* defines gospel as a kind of highly emotional religious music in four-part harmony that has developed mainly in African-American churches. The *Encyclopaedia Britannica* says that gospel is a form of black American music that came from worship services and from spiritual and blues singing. Ultimately, gospel reached white audiences and white churches as well. It spread largely through recordings and concerts on radio during the dark days of the Great Depression in the 1930s.

Gospel is more than simply a musical form, however. It is part of a black culture whose roots go back centuries in Africa. It is part of a legacy preserved by descendants of slaves whose passionate melodies grew out of misery and hope. It is part of white culture, of white churches and mixed congregations. It is uniquely American, yet somewhat hard to define. The study of gospel music provides a history lesson, a portrait of a people, and a religious sermon rolled into one. If you listen to its soul, if your feet move to its rhythm, it will take you back to a continent far away and then whirl you, clapping and singing, smack into the 21st century.

Members of a gospel choir raise their hands heavenward as they perform at a gospel revival. Many of gospel's trademark characteristics rise from the diverse history of black America.

off debts, and kidnapping kept the slave trade flourishing for a time.

Ancient India had slaves from about the first century B.C., and slavery was practiced in other parts of Asia as well. India had about eight million slaves in the mid-19th century when the British took over as a colonial power and abolished the practice.

Ancient Egypt and Mesopotamia also had slaves. In ancient Greece and Rome slavery was an accepted part of life. In fact, the first known major slave society existed in Athens. Perhaps a third of the population was enslaved from the fifth through the third centuries B.C. Indeed, slaves were responsible for the wealth and high standard of living in Athens and for most of the leisure time that the rich enjoyed. The Athenian slave society was all but wiped out about 338 B.C. when Philip II of Macedon conquered the Greeks and freed many of the captives.

Many of the slaves in ancient Athens and Rome were "losers" in the endless wars of the period. In addition, wars among Arabs, Turks, and Christians greatly added to the slave population along the Arabian Peninsula. In the 15th century, the invading Spaniards forced Indians in South America to work in the mines and fields. When the native people quickly died from exposure to European diseases and overwork, the Spaniards imported slaves from Africa.

Slavery also appeared early in the New World possessions of Great Britain. The first permanent British settlement in America took hold at Jamestown, Virginia, in 1607. In August 1619, a Dutch frigate appeared in Jamestown harbor. When it sailed away, it left behind 20 black slaves.

Throughout the 1600s, relatively small numbers of African slaves continued to be imported into the British colonies. Toward the end of the century, the southern colonies began enacting laws designed to control the slave population. In essence these laws, called the Slave Codes, gave masters complete authority to treat their slaves as they saw fit. A slave who didn't cooperate or who attempted to escape could be whipped, branded, castrated—even beaten to death—and the master could not be prosecuted. In addition, the Slave Codes prohibited the granting of legal rights and protections to slaves. They were simply property.

Eventually, out of the misery and suffering of slaves—from their attempts to escape to their daily struggle to survive—would come the music that we call gospel. The words to one of the best-known early gospel songs express the profound hopelessness that was so common:

> Before I'd be a slave, I'll be buried in my grave
> And go home to my Lord and be free.

The reasons for the spread of slavery in America were economic. The English colonies prospered in the New World largely because growing cash crops, like tobacco and cotton, on large plantations became very profitable. But a successful plantation needed many workers. Slaves were the ultimate bargain; after all, they worked for the cost of feeding and clothing them.

The work on the plantation was to change dramatically after 1793, when Eli Whitney of Westboro, Massachusetts, invented the cotton gin—a machine that offered a faster, more efficient way to separate seeds from the cotton fiber. Before the cotton gin, seeds had to be extracted by hand, a slow and sticky process. The new machine greatly speeded up the process, and the demand for cheaper cotton suddenly exploded. Greater demand for cotton, especially for export to the European market, led to an increased need for slaves to work the plantations. By

An early American advertisement for the sale of slaves tells little of the suffering many Africans endured on the journey to the American colonies.

TO BE SOLD, on board the Ship *Bance-Island*, on tuesday the 6th of *May* next, at *Ashley-Ferry*; a choice cargo of about 250 fine healthy NEGROES, just arrived from the Windward & Rice Coast. —The utmost care has already been taken, and shall be continued, to keep them free from the least danger of being infected with the SMALL-POX, no boat having been on board, and all other communication with people from *Charles-Town* prevented. — *Austin, Laurens, & Appleby.*

N. B. Full one Half of the above Negroes have had the SMALL-POX in their own Country.

1850, about two-thirds of the slaves in America were at work in the cotton fields.

The slave trade began to flourish as never before. Actually, it became so successful that it was soon more profitable to trade slaves than it was to export the crops they grew. There had been about 2,000 slaves in Virginia in 1681. Less than 200 years later, the total slave population in America numbered some four million!

Most of the slave trade originated on the west coast of Africa in an area known as the Gold Coast or Ivory Coast. Today, this area includes the nations of Senegal, Gambia, Guinea, Sierra Leone, Liberia, Ivory Coast, Ghana, Togo, Benin, Nigeria, Cameroon, Gabon, Congo, and Congo Republic.

The natives from countless villages in this area were grabbed from their homes and their fields, taken away to be thrust into chains and stuffed

By the mid-1800s the majority of slaves in America worked in cotton fields in the South.

aboard sailing ships especially constructed for the transport of human cargo. The platforms below deck were built to carry as many slaves as possible. Since the captives were fed a sparse diet of potatoes and rice, and disease spread easily in the cramped and filthy ship's hold, it wasn't unusual for a vessel to arrive in the New World with only half of its original cargo alive.

Terrible as these conditions were, it was not in the best interests of those who dealt in the slave trade to let their captives die. Typical of the instructions given to departing slave ships were the words of Thomas Starks of London to the captain of the *Africa* as it was setting out with 450 slaves: "Make your Negroes cheerful and pleasant making them dance at the Beating of your Drums, etc." How cheerful they were

Under the watchful eye of the captain, Africans are loaded on board a slave ship for the passage to the Americas.

made is doubtful, but ship captains typically went to some lengths to ensure that their human cargo would survive the frightful journey. If the weather was good, the slaves were allowed up on deck to exercise. This sometimes took the form of dancing to the beat of a drum, which was probably a tin plate.

Although it was obvious that the exercise was good for business, why did the ship captains tolerate music and dance? For the same reason. As we know, the captains cared very little for the well-being of slaves and certainly not at all for their entertainment. All they wanted was to deposit their cargo in good condition at a specified location and get paid. Since music helped those goals, the slaves were allowed to play. Music seemed to lift the depression that might cause a slave to refuse to eat, become ill, and die, a bad business proposition since there was no money collected on a dead slave.

Even in their confined areas below deck, the slaves sang and sometimes danced, beating out rhythms on a tin kettle or pan. But they weren't only playing music. Sometimes they were talking to each other. Ship captains often did not realize that the beat of the drum was actually a kind of code. Not only could slaves communicate, but they could make plans, for instance, on how to escape.

That was the ship captain's great fear on the sea—a slave revolt. There were many during the years of the slave trade. Most failed, but they caused enough trouble to keep the fear alive. The most famous revolt took place in 1839 aboard the clipper ship *Amistad*. The cargo of Africans, destined for slavery in Cuba, took over the ship at sea and sailed it to Long Island, New York. The men were taken into custody and a court battle followed. Were the Africans the property of the vessel owners? Or did the slave trade violate international trade laws? Former U.S. president John Quincy Adams was among the prominent Americans who got involved for the defense. Eventually, the U.S. Supreme Court ruled that the Africans could return home. This dramatic tale was made into a 1997 movie entitled *Amistad*, which starred Morgan Freeman and Anthony Hopkins.

The captains of slave ships may well have tolerated music on board ship for another reason. The sea journey from Africa to America was long and boring. After the slave ship was loaded with its human cargo in West Africa, the journey, called the Middle Passage—usually to Brazil or an island in the Caribbean—took at least a few weeks and as long as several months, depending on the weather. Ship captains at some point realized that African music was lively and entertaining. Some captains even

Generally kept below decks during the voyage from Africa to the Caribbean, many slaves never saw the light of day. Yet many captains became fond of the lively music of Africa and asked their captives to sing.

requested songs from their prisoners. If the slaves refused, they were often beaten into complying.

Once the slave ships landed in the New World, the slaves were sold at auction in huge markets where the captives were paraded in front of prospective buyers. Usually, the slaves most in demand were healthy adult males. Once the auction ended, the slave owner took his new slaves home to begin the rest of their lives of forced servitude. Upon reaching the plantation, the slave went through a so-called period of seasoning in which he or she adjusted to the new, bewildering, often harsh surroundings. There were two outcomes to the seasoning period: the slave either succumbed to diseases encountered in the New World, or else survived.

Many of those who did survive grew even stronger. Some lived on memories, some on faith, some on thoughts of escape. And most all lived on music. It was in their heads and their hearts when the ships sailed away from their homelands, and it remained in heads and hearts all through the slave years in America. The songs that slaves sang while they worked in the fields through the long hot hours made their toil seem lighter and less painful. Their religious songs, called spirituals, gave them hope that there was something or someone more powerful than the masters who owned them and that a better day was coming.

The music that the slaves brought with them to the New World was very closely entwined with religious beliefs and practices—a mixture of the worship of gods, spirits of ancestors, and fate. Each region in Africa had its own particular form of religious music, closely tied to many ceremonies. If there was a festival, a marriage, a birth, a death, or a war, there was appropriate music to go with it. This remains true today.

African music often sounds odd to those hearing it for the first time. In Western music, for instance, a passage may contain several different rhythms, but they are generally played one at a time. African music may play two, three, or more at once. This generally gets sorted out by the largest drum, which keeps up a regular beat that does not vary. The drum is at the heart of the music of black Africa. There is an amazing variety of drums of varying sizes, some as small as 12 inches and some more than six feet long. Drums that stood upright on the ground were sometimes struck with the palms of the hands instead of sticks. Sometimes drum players wore bells around their wrists when they struck the drum surface, producing a loud jingling noise.

Other instruments used in the playing of African music included small flutes, usually with three holes and made of long, hollow reeds; horns of elephant tusks; trumpets of ivory and wood; and a small piano-

Often considered the heart of African music, drums were also used as a means of communication among slaves, which caused some slave owners to ban them. The drums seen here belong to an African performing group appearing at London's Royal Albert Hall.

like instrument. In modern Africa, this is known as a *sansa*, or thumb-piano.

One of the most lasting influences of the music of Africa in American gospel music today is the emphasis on the ensemble, or group of players, instead of solo performances. In churches, at festivals, at a backyard barbecue, everybody joins in. In the early days, only males played the instruments and the women sang and danced. Those who stood around watching clapped their hands and stamped their feet. For a successful musical festival in Africa, everybody took part, a feeling that remains true in America today.

Music, along with dance and religious practices, always remained of prime importance in the lives of slaves in America. It remains of prime importance in the lives of many black Americans today. That is because the roots are so deep. Music was, and is, a vital expression of life in Africa.

2

The Roots in Slavery

Sometimes I feel like a motherless child,
A long ways from home.

AS MANY AS 15 million Africans were brought as slaves to the Western Hemisphere. Most of them were sent to Brazil and the Caribbean islands, where they worked, and died in alarming numbers, in the sugarcane fields. Only about 1 of every 20 slaves imported found his or her way to the 13 growing British colonies and the French colony of Louisiana. The number would steadily grow—with most of the slaves coming to the United States between 1741 and 1808—until the Civil War ended the shameful practice once and for all.

As the colonies grew, the need for workers increased, and the so-called Slave Codes came into effect. Basic to the codes was the concept that slaves were property, not persons. If you could accept that premise, then you could sell slaves just as you would sell anything else you owned—a horse, perhaps, or a house. Furthermore, there were laws protecting property owners. Just as someone stealing a horse would be punished, so too would someone stealing a slave. It was all a question of property.

But, of course, slaves were real people whose lives had been torn apart forever. How did they endure? Against all odds, their spirit often proved astounding.

A young girl sings while other members of her gospel choir clap and sing along with her. Gospel's tradition of ensemble singing has its roots in the music of slaves working the fields of New World plantations.

23

In an effort to keep their sanity and some sense of what they had left behind, they turned to one thing that could not be taken from them—their music.

Somehow, out of this ability to endure through music, came the absurd, twisted notion of "happy singing slaves" that persisted well beyond the Civil War. Perhaps it was a belief created to soothe whites' consciences. One of the most famous songs to keep alive the contented slave theme was "My Old Kentucky Home," sung most notably before the Kentucky Derby horse race each May at Churchill Downs in Louisville. The original lyric, no longer sung in public, contained these lines:

> Oh, the sun shines bright in the old Kentucky home
> 'Tis summer, the darkies are gay.

It was written by Stephen Foster, a white man, in 1853.

As the slave trade prospered, the large numbers of Africans who were brought to America came with different kinds of music. Taking from the four-part harmony of their native lands, slaves in the New World eventually blended their music to produce a smooth-flowing, emotional story of sorrow and suffering, loneliness and hope. This music would in time become the uniquely American musical form known as the Negro spiritual, a kind of English-language folk hymn.

A spin-off of the spiritual, which ultimately had a place in gospel music, were the *shout songs*. Strictly speaking, they were not considered spirituals. In a variation called a *ring shout*, groups or church congregations moved, clapped, and shouted to a beat, repeating a line of rhythmic lyric for hours on end. Not only did the ring shout eventually become part of gospel music, but it also became part of the 20th century when the Beatles recorded a song entitled "Twist and Shout." Few who enjoyed the song knew of its origins.

The singing and dancing of slaves was often misinterpreted by their white owners as a sign of happiness and contentment. Stephen Foster encouraged this belief in the lyrics of his song My Old Kentucky Home.

As the years passed, the descendants of the first black slaves became less and less African and more and more part of the country into which they had been born. This was their home. It was here they would live and die and fight for freedom. And it was here that they would establish their own music—a form that would grow and strengthen and diversify. It would eventually become an integral part of the American scene, but it would always remain uniquely African American.

African slaves were not the only newcomers to America to arrive with musical traditions, of course. The colonists themselves brought their own music, mainly from England. Concerts, balls, and musical evenings were all part of the colonial social scene. There was a great demand for entertainment, and, especially on the southern plantations, blacks were often called upon to provide it. In fact, sometimes slaves who worked in the main house (rather than in the fields) were encouraged to learn new musical instruments or develop a new musical skill, which in turn could be used to entertain the white household or impress the master's guests. It was not unusual for advertisements about slave sales to note that an individual could, for example, play the violin or the French horn.

Before the American Revolution, some music was actually published in the colonies. Most of it consisted of hymns and church music, some written by a noted composer of American folk music, William Billings (1746–1800) of Boston. A good deal of the music of the time, however, was not written, but passed from place to place, people to people. Black musicians, present at various musical gatherings in the colonies, heard the music of Great Britain and Europe. Over time, they incorporated the violin and other European instruments into the music they had brought from Africa.

Probably the best musical job held by a slave belonged to Sy Gilliant, whose master was Lord Botecourt. Gilliant was the official fiddler at the state balls in Williamsburg, Virginia. Noted for his courtly manners, he wore fancy embroidered clothes and shoes with large buckles. After the state capital moved to Richmond, Gilliant was assisted in his musical tasks by London Brigs, who was said to be quite proficient on the clarinet and flute.

Plantation work was hard for everyone involved, white and black, slave and free. So any reason to take a few hours off was eagerly awaited. Almost anything—holidays, birthdays, house raisings, weddings, births—was cause for music, usually a banjo or fiddle and usually provided by the plantation's slaves. When the banjo sprang to life, people began to dance. Early on, it was evident that white people recognized the influence of blacks on American music. There are early references to "negro tunes," and one dance was called the "Negro Jig."

In some areas of the colonies, especially where there were large concentrations of slaves, so-called slave festivals were held. The slaves were given some time off to gather for music and dancing, which might last for several days. The music provided for these festivals came from homemade drums and other instruments. One was the *banjar*, brought from Africa. Thomas Jefferson wrote about the instrument in *Notes on Virginia*, his only book, published in France before he became president. Jefferson describes the banjar, which became known as the banjo, as being the forerunner of the guitar. Others dispute this, however. The banjar as Jefferson would have seen it was a scooped-out large gourd, cut to attach a handle. The drumhead was a coonskin stretched over the bowl of the gourd, with four strings near the center of the drum and attached to the handle. The strings were made of any handy material.

Slaves found brief moments of relief from the hardships of their lives in celebrations such as holidays and weddings. These occasions almost always included music, singing, and dancing.

A man stands before a gospel group playing a washtub bass while another man plays a banjo. Both instruments can trace their origins back to early gospel music.

Many instruments found their way from Africa into American black music. One was an odd creation called the *bafolo*, a kind of distant cousin to the xylophone. Another was the earth bow, used in western and central Africa. The influence of these early instruments has steadily trickled down through the years. Black street bands today usually have a washtub bass, also known simply as the "tub." It's actually an inverted washtub with an upright broomstick attached to it. The musician plucks a string that is attached between the upper end of the stick and the tub.

It may seem odd that slave owners allowed time off for festivals or, for that matter, any "light-hearted" singing in the plantation fields. The truth is, like the ship captains, plantation owners really didn't care what the slaves did as far as music, singing, or any other pastimes were concerned—unless, of course, it interfered with plantation work or interrupted the life of the plantation. Slaves were generally allowed to make their own musical instruments. Drums, however, were frequently an exception, since the masters had finally caught on to—perhaps from the ship captains—the use of the drum as a means of signaling.

Over the course of many years, the music that would become gospel and the music of the Old World blended. The powerful emotions brought about by slavery and the loss of one's homeland began to give a new, uniquely American dimension to what was originally the music of Africa.

HYMN OF THE FREEDMAN
RESPECTFULLY DEDICATED TO MRS. COL. CHAS. W. FRIB

3

Music Goes to War

Oh, I want to be in that number,
When the saints go marching in.

Members of an African-American unit, with their white commanding officer, are depicted before a Union encampment. Although many blacks fought both for and against England during the American Revolution, it was not until the Civil War that the first black regiments would officially appear.

BLACKS IN AMERICA have a long history of fighting for their country, even when it was not their country. A few fought in the French and Indian War between 1754 and 1763, a worldwide battle between France and Great Britain that was fought over control of the vast colonial territory in North America. The British finally won, but in doing so they ran up burdensome war debts. Ironically, this planted the seeds of unrest that would result in the American Revolution a little more than a decade later.

Some 5,000 blacks fought in the American Revolution between 1775 and 1783, as the United States declared itself free from Great Britain. Why did they fight? Why would they want to? Not all blacks in America were slaves, of course, and they fought for the same reasons people have been fighting for centuries—for freedom, for justice, for the promise of a better life. Although there were laws against blacks in the military, some of the colonies did induct slaves with the understanding that they would be granted their freedom at war's end—if they survived.

Not all blacks in the American Revolution fought for the colonies, however. In 1775, George

Washington imposed a ban on recruiting black men. But the British had another idea. Lord Dunsmore, the commander of British forces in Virginia, issued a proclamation stating that any slave who joined the British military would be guaranteed his freedom at war's end. It must be remembered that back in 1775, it did not seem as though the poorly equipped and trained colonial military stood any chance against the overwhelming power of the British Empire. And in any event, slaves were not likely to have much loyalty to either side. Some of the slaves decided to go where freedom seemed most likely, and a number joined the British.

This, naturally, alarmed the colonies, so they began to recruit blacks as well. One of the most dramatic of these recruitments was an entire battalion of slaves from Rhode Island. They fought in upstate New York and at the Battle of Yorktown, which ended the war. The only colonies that refused to recruit blacks were Georgia and South Carolina. Of all the southern colonies, these were the most committed to the "peculiar institution" of slavery.

Not surprisingly, many blacks in the colonial military were assigned to musical duties. Every regiment needed a fife and drum, after all, to keep marching time. And many of the slaves had the appropriate musical talents. In the Virginia military, black recruits were employed specifically as "drummers or fifers." Many of the war songs of the American Revolution were composed by blacks, but few of them were written down and so few remain. Any song would have had a hard time competing with the "hit" war tune anyway. It was "Yankee Doodle," composer unknown, and it kept the regiments stepping lively.

Ironically, the first American to fall in the fight for America's independence was a black man; some historians say he was both African and Natick Indian. His name was Crispus Attucks, and little is

Crispus Attucks, the first man to fall in the fight for America's independence, died during the Boston Massacre in 1770. Today a statue commemorating Attucks's death can be seen in Boston Common, a large park in the city's center.

known about him except that he was perhaps a runaway slave. In 1750, an advertisement appeared in Framingham, Massachusetts, for the recovery of a runaway slave presumed to be Attucks. Nothing is known of him for the next 20 years. But on the evening of March 5, 1770, Attucks led about 50 colonial protesters to the British garrison in Boston. A fight started between the soldiers and colonials. In what became known as the Boston Massacre, the soldiers killed five colonists, Attucks being the first. This incident was another step on the road to revolution. All five victims were buried in one grave. A monument honoring Attucks stands in Boston Common.

After the American Revolution ended in 1783, blacks who had served in the military were granted freedom. But slavery was alive and growing. However, even before the war, those opposed to slavery had been crying for legislation against it. In 1808, Congress passed a law prohibiting the importation of African slaves. Slavery slowly died in the North, but in the southern states it became even more firmly rooted.

The music on the plantations continued pretty much as before. For the white owners, it might have been entertainment, but for the black workers, it was at least a small relief from misery. However, as the years passed, there were signs of unrest and occasional slave revolts. Because of that, African instruments themselves were often banned, although they never did disappear entirely.

In the War of 1812, the former colonies and Britain fought again. The dispute was chiefly over British interference with U.S. trade on the high seas. British ships often stopped U.S. vessels on the high seas and took the crew, claiming that the men were deserters from the Royal Navy.

Black Americans fought in this war, too, though their numbers were smaller than during the Revolution. It is difficult to quote exact figures because the

Two members of an all-black Civil War regiment take aim from behind the safety of a building. Close to 180,000 black Americans fought for the Union during the Civil War.

records of servicemen during that time usually did not refer to race. As in the American Revolution, some slaves joined the British side with the promise of freedom. Most of those who joined the American side were in the U.S. Navy, probably because at the beginning of the fighting the army refused to take them.

In 1814, General Andrew Jackson issued a proclamation that allowed blacks to join the army. Some of them fought in important battles, especially in Louisiana near the end of the conflict. One group, known as the "colored Creoles" of Louisiana, fought in the Battle of New Orleans on January 8, 1815. Supposedly, they had their own fight song in French, which translated as "Go forward, grenadiers; he who is dead requires no ration."

There are very few references to black soldiers during the war. Jordan Little is said to have drummed the men into battle lines during the fight for New Orleans, and the name of drummer Jordan B. Noble is praised for his work with the Seventh Regiment of Infantry. There is a record of three black musician-sailors during the war: Jessie Wall, who played the fife on the frigate *Niagara*, George Brown, a bugler on the *Chesapeake*, and another fifer, Cyrus Tiffany, on the *Alliance*. Interestingly, quite a few all-black brass bands appeared in big cities right after the war; many probably got their experience in the military.

Thousands of black Americans fought in the Civil War. The North put about 180,000 into uniform; some 32,000 died. About 18,000 black men served in the U.S. Navy. Black soldiers faced not only the threat of death, but the prejudice of their fellow soldiers. Northerners may have been fighting for the abolishment of slavery, but they were rarely willing to serve side by side with a black man. Although black soldiers were frequently given the most menial jobs or allowed to play the drum marching into battle, most fought with great honor and distinction. Twenty-one black Americans won the Congressional Medal of Honor, the newly created highest award for military service.

It may seem strange, but blacks—some slaves and some free men—also served in the Confederate army during the Civil War. They were generally given the jobs of cooks, servants, or musicians. As the war was nearing an end and the South feared defeat, the Confederacy passed a law that allowed black soldiers to enlist. None saw combat before the war ended.

4

Gospel Goes to Church

Gimme that old time religion,
It's good enough for me.

EVEN IN THE early colonial years, white owners took their slaves to church—to the white church, of course. The colonists were quite righteous about everyone having religion. It's likely, however, they were not as concerned with saving black souls as they were with preventing trouble. It was widely felt that a churchgoing slave would not be so inclined to revolt. For instance, in an Episcopalian church in Williamsburg, Virginia, several hundred slaves were baptized. Whether church members or not, blacks were often part of the congregation and joined in the services and the singing, especially the singing of psalms. The slaves were segregated by color and gender: black men and women apart from the white congregation, and black men apart from black women.

Slaves in the northern colonies were often taken in as part of the household, albeit not on an equal level. They were sometimes given the last name of

In an example that harkens back to gospel's roots, a group of men sing as an ensemble. One of the main characteristics of gospel music is the participation of every performer, whether by singing, dancing, or simply clapping along with the beat.

the master of the household. Some of these British names continue to be passed on through generations of black Americans. In those cases, the slaves, or servants, were generally baptized into the church of the master.

In reality, most clergymen in America considered slaves as well as Native Americans to be heathens—technically defined as a person who does not acknowledge the God of the Bible. However, in colonial America, as elsewhere, heathen also meant someone from an "inferior culture." Thus it became the duty of the clergy to convert these heathens to Christianity. And they tried, often with great zeal and often with great success, at least on the surface.

The established churches to which most of the clergy and colonists belonged had their roots in the formal services of England. The rather confining atmosphere of Episcopalians, Presbyterians, and Catholics was not one in which the music of Africa could readily flourish. Therefore, it is not surprising that when freedom came, most former slaves turned to other churches, such as Methodists and Baptists, where they could express their emotions and fervor.

In general, Baptists shared the same beliefs as most Protestants. However, they held that only adult believers in the faith should be baptized by being immersed in water. Although the Baptist movement came out of England, its origins in the United States stem from Roger Williams, an advocate of religious liberty who established a Baptist church in Providence, Rhode Island, after the Puritans forced him out of the Massachusetts Bay Colony.

Baptists in the United States did not unite into one body until 1814, but factions eventually developed over the issue of slavery. Today, Southern Baptists and Northern Baptists differ in various aspects of the religion.

Although the Baptist church services were appealing to black Americans, they formed their own churches. Several of the churches organized by freed slaves after the Civil War—among them the African Methodist Episcopal (AME) Church and the African Methodist Episcopal Zion (AMEZ) Church—still exist today. These churches have contributed enormously to the culture and character of black life in America and it is there, probably more than any other place, that gospel music flourishes.

The slaves also attended prayers and psalm singing in their master's home and prayer meetings in their area. In addition, there were weddings and funerals during which the slaves took part in the singing. Eventually, some of the singing of psalms began to become part of the slaves' own services as well.

During this period, psalm singing was rather solemn until the reform movement decided to change things. An organ and chorus began to jazz up the church service. In the 18th century, hymns became part of the church program.

After the American Revolution, a freed slave, Newport Gardner (1746–1826), may have been the first black American to open a music school. After buying freedom for himself and his family in 1791, Gardner opened his school in Newport, Rhode Island. He had spent his early years there in the service of the Gardner family. Mrs. Sarah Ann Gardner had recognized his musical talent and arranged for him to study outside the home. When Gardner opened his school, Mrs. Gardner became his pupil.

Gardner became a deacon in the First Congregational Church and later organized the Newport Colored Union Church and Society. He also went to Africa as a missionary.

Gardner composed many church hymns, including "Hear the Lord, O Ye African race / Hear the words of promise."

For a time after the American Revolution, a number of music schools run by blacks for blacks were opened. Besides lessons in church singing, there were instructions in brass and other instruments. Black independent churches began to form, bringing in the new music. But as the Civil War neared, these churches were on shaky ground, viewed as a danger to the institution of slavery.

By the middle of the 19th century, gospel music was emerging once again to meet the needs of the people. Born out of rural campfire songs, where thousands sat to listen to a traveling preacher, the new gospel came into the cities where the population was rapidly growing. In open fields or under circus tents, people listened to a new gospel, borrowed from slave songs and folk songs and given a little hype by Tin Pan Alley. "A Great Camp Meetin' " is an example of a spiritual that might have been sung at a large outdoor gathering:

> Oh, walk togedder, children, don't you get a-weary
> Walk togedder, children, Don't you get weary
> Walk togedder, children, Don't you get a-weary,
> Dere's a great camp meetin' in de promised land.
> Gwine to mourn an' nebber tire, mourn an' nebber tire,
> Mourn an' nebber tire; Dere's a great camp meetin' in
>   the promised land.

The person most responsible for this new direction in music was Thomas Andrew Dorsey, called the Father of Gospel Music. Among the hundreds of songs he wrote are "Peace in the Valley" and "Take My Hand, Precious Lord."

Dorsey was born in Villa Rica, Georgia, in 1899. His father was an itinerant Baptist preacher. By the time Dorsey was in his teens, he was an accomplished blues pianist—not an easy task since the family home held no piano. He was so determined to learn that he walked some eight miles back and forth to his piano teacher four times a week.

Although he was soon making money by playing at local dance halls and bars, Dorsey moved north to Chicago in 1921. He formed his own band, married,

Thomas A. Dorsey, "the Father of Gospel Music," plays the piano. Dorsey, who died in 1993, is regarded as one of the most prolific and gifted gospel composers in music history.

and joined the Pilgrim Baptist Church. Although he tried writing church music, he was often lured by the sound of blues and jazz. During this period, he went on a tour that he organized for blues singer Ma Rainey. But in 1932, his wife and infant son died. Dorsey was now back in the church full time with his first religious compositions, "Some Day—Some Where" and "If You See My Savior."

Although fully dedicated to the publication of religious music, Dorsey found it hard to sell his songs. So he decided to do what popular songwriters do—promote himself and his tunes. He traveled from church to church singing to the congregations. Eventually, black Americans responded to his music. In all, Dorsey wrote and published more than 400 songs and inspired countless recording artists—from country singers Eddie Arnold and Johnny Cash to the great Mahalia Jackson, pop idol Elvis Presley, and modern stars Aretha Franklin and Gladys Knight.

Dorsey said that when he reached Chicago in the 1920s, the music compositions closest to gospel were evangelistic songs. It was Dorsey who claimed to have coined the term *gospel songs* after he heard a group of five people singing on a Sunday morning in Chicago.

Dorsey received many honors during his lifetime, including being the first black American inducted into the Nashville Hall of Fame, which honors country music. In 1982, Thomas Dorsey's life was chronicled in *Say Amen, Somebody*, a wonderful documentary that also presented the life of Willie Mae Ford Smith, another gospel legend. Thomas Dorsey, who had well earned the title Father of Gospel Music, died in 1993, at the ripe old age of 94.

The singer who came to be called the Queen of the Gospel Song and the greatest gospel singer of all time was Mahalia Jackson. Her powerful cathedral voice was simply extraordinary, and her singing was pure soul. She often claimed not to need a micro-phone: "Just open the windows and the doors. And let the sound pour out."

Jackson was born into a poor New Orleans water-front family in 1911. Her mother died when she was five. Although surrounded by the rich development of new kinds of music, she remained focused only on gospel. She almost had to be. From the age of five, she began to sing in her father's church choir. He worked on the docks during the day, cut hair at night, and was a preacher on Sundays. That was the most impor-tant part. He would allow no music but gospel in the house.

From an early age, it was obvious that Mahalia Jackson had a very powerful voice. She was so impres-sive that her father's cousins, who were traveling with the legendary Ma Rainey, wanted her to go along on their road tour. Her father was outraged. His influ-

The Queen of the Gospel Song, Mahalia Jackson, made her first gospel recording with the help of Thomas A. Dorsey. Jackson's music would in turn inspire such artists as Billie Holiday and Aretha Franklin.

ence was so strong that in adult life, Jackson refused to sing blues or jazz and concentrated solely on gospel. However, she did admit to a great fondness for the Mother of the Blues, Bessie Smith, and her recording of "Careless Love."

After completing the eighth grade, Jackson went to work as a laundress. But she had no intention of staying in New Orleans. By the age of 16, she had saved enough money to make it to Chicago, where she lived with an aunt in the city's South Side, which had a large black community. Jackson joined the Greater Salem Baptist Church and formed a group called the Johnson Gospel Singers. Before long, she began to sing on her own. In 1934, with the help of Thomas Dorsey, she made her first recording, "God's Gonna Separate the Wheat from the Tare." It was not a financial success. So her husband, Ike, whom she married in 1935, urged her to sing more-popular songs. She refused and vowed to stay solely with gospel.

Jackson proved that she knew what was best for herself, although it was a long pull. It wasn't until 1946 that she came up with a hit recording, "I Will Move on Up a Little Higher." It sold nearly two million copies. But the people who bought the record were mostly black. She was still little known in the white community. That changed after a white professor of music in New York City heard the recording and invited Jackson to sing at a concert in Tanglewood, Massachusetts. From then on, her fame spread. Thomas Dorsey also acted as her mentor, and Jackson helped to popularize many of his gospel songs. The world was soon amazed with the depth and richness of her contralto voice. She first appeared in New York City's famed Carnegie Hall in 1950; three more packed concerts would follow. Radio and television tours both home and abroad brought her amazing voice to millions. She sang on the *Ed Sullivan Show*. In 1958, she appeared with legend Duke Ellington at the Newport Jazz Festival in Rhode Island for his gospel interlude *Black, Brown, and Beige*. She performed at the inauguration of four U.S. presidents: Harry S. Truman, Dwight D. Eisenhower, John F. Kennedy, and Lyndon B. Johnson. No stranger to the evils of segregation, she joined the civil rights movement in the 1950s, and she sang on the steps of the Lincoln Memorial in 1963 when Martin Luther King Jr. gave his memorable "I Have a Dream" speech.

Mahalia Jackson died in 1972 of heart disease. Although constantly urged to lend her glorious voice to other forms, she never compromised her vision of gospel and its place in music and religion. Gospel music, she said, "preceded jazz, affected jazz, gave it inspiration and new forms. But jazz did not affect gospel. That inspiration came from the Lord."

Another great gospel voice that took a different route belonged to Rosetta Tharpe (1921–1973) of Cotton Plant, Arkansas. She was the first black

Rosetta "Sister" Tharpe was the first black gospel performer to appear at the legendary Apollo Theater. Tharpe took gospel beyond its traditional roots and helped expose the music to a wider audience.

American to take gospel out of the church and into a popular setting. Later known as Sister Tharpe, she began touring professionally, singing and playing the guitar, at the age of six. Whereas Mahalia Jackson felt that gospel should stay "pure," Tharpe wanted it brought into the mainstream. She did so in 1938 by appearing in a Cab Calloway show at the famed Cotton Club in Harlem. The following year she became the first gospel artist to record for a major record label, Decca. She was the first black gospel singer to tour extensively in Europe and the first to sing gospel at New York's Apollo Theater. She also appeared at Carnegie Hall and the Newport Folk Festival. Although her appearance in nightclubs often offended many of those who, like Jackson, wanted gospel to remain separate from popular music, Tharpe is credited with bringing an appreciation of this music to millions.

5

Negro Spirituals

Nobody knows the trouble I've seen,
Nobody knows but Jesus.

THE SPIRITUAL IS a religious folk song, an emotional music created by black people, not for them. The raw materials for spirituals came from the Bible, from nature, and from the personal experiences of blacks in America. The spiritual may trace its roots to Africa, but it has been influenced by European musical styles as well. Just as sailors made up sea chanteys while they worked, so plantation slaves composed spirituals to make their burdens lighter. These songs gave them courage when they felt they had none, and the music was also a way to pass what little free time was allowed. Many spirituals contained biblical themes reflecting the slaves' hope for freedom, or at least a better life beyond this one. The freedom theme is expressed in the well-known spiritual "Go Down, Moses," in which the leader of Hebrew slaves is beseeched to seek the Egyptian pharaoh and demand freedom for his people. The theme of release in an afterlife is found in

With the lead singer temporarily silent, three background vocalists sing exuberantly, reflecting the call-and-response technique popular in spirituals. Gospel music takes much of its inspiration from spirituals and the raw power of faith.

many spirituals—among them, "Swing Low, Sweet Chariot" and "Deep River."

These folk spirituals, sometimes also called jubilees, shouts, or work songs, took a special musical form known as call and response. Throughout a song, individual singers make up new verses (the call), which are answered by the entire group (the chorus singing the response). In this way, the singing of a spiritual could go on for quite some time, depending on the size of the group. Here is an example of a simple, short-phrase call-and-response form of spiritual. The title is "What You Going to Do When the Lamp Burns Down?" Note the different parts for group leader and choir, or chorus:

> LEADER: Oh, poor sinner,
> CHOIR: Now is your time,
> LEADER: Oh, poor sinner,
> CHOIR: Now is your time,
> LEADER: Oh, poor sinner,
> CHOIR: Now is your time, What you going to do
>   when your lamp burns down?
> LEADER: Oh the lamp burns down and you cannot see,
> Chorus: What you going to do when your lamp burns
>   down?

The following is a long-phrase call-and-response spiritual, called "Lord, Until I Reach My Home":

> CHOIR: Until I reach my home, until I reach my
>   home, I never 'spect to give the journey
>   over, until I reach my home. [Repeat]
> LEADER: Old Satan's mighty busy, he follows my night
>   and day, and ev'ry time I go to pray, I find
>   him in my way. [Repeat]

And this is a combination of the two forms, called "I Am Seeking for a City":

> LEADER: I am seeking for a city
> CHOIR: Hallelujah, I am seeking for a city, Hallelujah.
> LEADER: For a city into the heaven

CHOIR: Hallelujah. For a city into the heaven,
               Hallelujah.
          Lord, I don't feel noways tired, Oh, glory,
               Hallelujah;
          O hope to shout glory when this world is on
               fire,
          Oh, glory, Hallelujah.

Although the expression of sorrow is at the heart of much gospel, during the Civil War this music became a rallying cry of sorts. It was often part of the code that led many on the road to freedom. During these years, music was an aid to the runaway slaves escaping to the North by means of the Underground Railroad:

The gospel train is coming
I hear it close at hand
Get on board children
Get on board.

Neither underground nor a railroad, the Underground Railroad got its name because its activities were carried out secretly, and because it used a language based on railroad terms: stopping places along the way were called stations, the slaves themselves were spoken of as packages or freight; those who helped them were known as conductors. No one knows for sure how many slaves gained freedom through the Underground Railroad, but its very existence won sympathy for the plight of blacks. When Harriet Beecher Stowe wrote *Uncle Tom's Cabin*—perhaps the most well-known story about slavery—she obtained firsthand knowledge of how the Railroad worked from members she knew in Cincinnati, Ohio.

Throughout the period that the Underground Railroad operated—from about 1850 until the Civil War—music was a large part of its operation. Songs such as "I Am Bound for the Land of Canaan," or "Steal Away to Jesus," or "I Don't Expect to Stay Much Longer Here" reflected the profound dramas of the era. Some conductors used their own particular

Harriet Tubman, seen to the far left holding a wash pan, was one of the conductors of the Underground Railroad. Like Tubman, many conductors would use music to give slaves fleeing to the North cues and instructions.

songs to alert possible runaways. For instance, one of the most famous of the Railroad conductors was former slave Harriet Tubman (ca. 1820–1913). When she made a trip into the South to lead slaves to freedom, she is said to have sung a special song informing those who wanted to escape that she was a conductor and would lead them to freedom:

> Dark and thorny is de pathway
> Where de pilgrim makes his ways

If an escape was being planned, a conductor might sing or play such songs as "Brother Moses Gone to de Promised Land," or "Good News, de Chariot's Coming." Some songs told the slaves what to do. "Follow the Drinkin' Gourd," for example, advised a runaway to keep moving with an eye on the constellation known as the Big Dipper. The two stars at the front of the Dipper's bowl point to the North Star, which is always north in the night sky and thus could guide runaway slaves in their flight to freedom.

After the Civil War, when former slaves began to meet in their own churches, they brought with them many of the Protestant hymns they had sung in white churches. But now the hymns took on a new life. Filled with emotional depth and charged rhythm, these spirituals became a way of letting out emotions and feelings. In the country, spiritual singing could be heard for miles around on a Sunday morning. Whites in the area had never heard anything quite like it before.

But the singing of spirituals was more than a religious show put on for entertainment. Meaning and understanding flowed through the words. Former slaves knew exactly what they meant when they sang these lyrics:

> Deep river, my home is over Jordan,
> Deep river, Lord, I want to cross over into campground.
> Oh, chillun, Oh, don't you want to go, to that gospel
>   feast,
> That promised land, where all is peace?
> Walk into heaven, and take my seat
> And cast my crown at Jesus' feet
> Lord, I want to cross over into campground.

They also understood the special meaning of

> Go down, Moses, way down in Egypt land
> Tell ole Pharaoh, To let my people go.

Perhaps they could look into the future when they sang

> I'm a goin' to tell you 'bout de comin' of de Saviour
> Fare you well, Fare you well,
> In dat great gittin' up mornin'
> Fare you well, Fare you well.

Music in black churches after the Civil War became a large part of the identity of African Americans. These hymns, sung at church services, weddings, baptisms, and funerals, came to be included in *Slave Songs of the United States*, the first collection of black spirituals, which was originally published in 1867. The editors of this book—William Francis Allen, Charles Pickard Ware, and Lucy McKim Garrison—offered this observation: "It is difficult to express the entire character of these negro ballads by mere musical notes and signs. The odd turns made in the throat and the curious rhythmic effect produced by single voices chiming in at different irregular intervals seem almost as impossible to place on the score as the singing of birds or the tones of an aeolian harp." Included in the collection is a popular rowing song that is a plea to the Archangel Michael:

> Michael row de boat ashore, Hallelujah!
> Michael boat a gospel boat, Hallelujah!

Also included in *Slave Songs* are such well-known favorites as "Blow Your Trumpet, Gabriel," "I Hear from Heaven Today," and "Roll, Jordan, Roll," the latter being the first black American spiritual believed to appear in print with its music, published in Philadelphia in 1862 by Lucy McKim. The second spiritual published with music is said to be "Done Wid Driber's Dribin'," which appeared in *The Continental Monthly* a year later. It is especially interesting because some of its verses, such as "Done wid Massa's hollerin' " and "Done wid Missus' scoldin'," make it one of the very few spirituals to refer to freeing the slaves.

This unique type of music took a giant leap beyond local church services with the help of one singing group and two black composers. The group came from the Fisk School, which would later become Fisk University, in Nashville, Tennessee. This college for blacks, opened in 1866 about six months after the end of the Civil War, was founded by three white men: John Ogden, Edward T. Smith, and Erastus Cravath. The school was named for a white benefactor, General Clinton B. Fisk of the Tennessee Freedmen's Bureau, who gave the new school the former Union army barracks near present-day Nashville Union Station. The school's first students all shared common experiences of poverty and slavery.

George L. White, another white man and a U.S. army officer, was hired by the school as treasurer, music professor, and choirmaster. As part of his work, he formed a group of singers known as the Nashville Students. Although White intended that the group perform classical music both in Nashville and neighboring towns, he asked that each concert end with a spiritual. Within a short time, the Nashville Students developed into a first-rate singing group.

But the school was in trouble and Fisk was running out of money. That should not have been too surprising. Southern whites in general were not enthusiastic about the establishment of all-black schools after the Civil War. In addition, the Ku Klux Klan was in full force, destroying schools that had been built for blacks and murdering those who had helped to establish them.

So, in 1871, George White decided to take the Nashville Students—now renamed the Fisk Jubilee Singers—on the road to raise money for their university. They would become the first group to perform spirituals throughout the world. Along with two teachers, 11 Fisk students—6 women and 5 men, who were all from slave families—left the campus in October 1871.

They included the following individuals:

- Isaac Dickerson was born a slave in Wytheville, Virginia, in 1850; he had been a hotel waiter and a teacher before entering Fisk.

Members of the Fisk Jubilee Singers pose on a railroad platform before leaving Nashville to perform in London for the queen of England. The success of the Fisk Jubilee Singers helped raise funds for Jubilee Hall, the first permanent building in the United States erected specifically for the education of blacks. Today it is a National Historical Landmark.

- Green Evans, born in 1848, was a former slave and the most widely traveled of the group; after two years as a servant for a Yankee office in Selma, Alabama, he taught school and then entered Fisk.
- Jennie Jackson, the granddaughter of one of President Andrew Jackson's servants, was born free, although her mother was a slave; she entered Fisk in 1866.
- Maggie Porter was born a slave in Lebanon, Tennessee, in 1853; because her mother was a favorite servant in a wealthy house, she saw little of the cruelty of slavery.

- Ella Sheppard was born a slave but her father bought his freedom for $1,800 and his daughter's freedom for $350; the master refused to free her mother. Sheppard was considered the backbone of the singing group.

To this day, the entire college pauses each October 6 to honor the anniversary of the singers' departure for their initial tour. And the Fisk Jubilee Singers still tour every year.

When the Fisk troupe gave its first concert, mostly of classical music, in Cincinnati, it did not go well. No one had heard of the group, so few turned out. With little money and thin clothing against the cold northern winter, they kept on. Often they were denied hotel rooms or were chased out of railroad stations because they were black. However, in Oberlin, Ohio, the group was asked to sing at a convention of Congregational Church ministers. White decided to include some spirituals, against the wishes of most of the singers, who thought they'd be laughed at. In spite of such reservations, the group sang "Steal Away to Jesus" and the audience was enchanted.

The Fisk Jubilee Singers soon became an "overnight" success. By the time they reached Brooklyn, New York, a concert had been arranged for them by Congregational minister Henry Ward Beecher, an outspoken opponent of slavery, whose sister was Harriet Beecher Stowe, author of Uncle Tom's Cabin. After the concert, the Fisk singers became the toast of New York City. They later sang at the White House for President Ulysses S. Grant.

On their tour, the Fisk Jubilee Singers earned $20,000 for their school. For the next seven years, they performed throughout the United States and in Europe. The playbill from one of their performances during their European tour in 1874 read: "The Jubilee Singers, ex-slave students from Fisk University, Nashville, Tennessee, U.S.A., will give a Service of Song consisting of Slave Hymns & Melodies in the Exchange Opera House, Wolverhampton." During this tour, the singers raised another $150,000. With some of the money, the university constructed Jubilee Hall, the first permanent building erected in the United States for educating black students. Today it is a designated National Historical Landmark building.

Three years after the Fisk Jubilee Singers began touring, a group from Hampton Institute in Hampton, Virginia, went north on the same mission to deliver the same music. It too met with great success and was followed by choirs from Tuskegee Institute in Alabama and other schools. Besides raising money for their schools, such performances spread the sound and feeling of the spiritual. Today, similar groups still perform throughout the United States, although their repertoire has generally shifted away from spirituals and now includes all kinds of music.

The first recognized composer of gospel hymns was a traveling preacher named Charles A. Tindley. Born in Maryland in 1859, he studied for the ministry in Philadelphia, where he founded the East Calvary Methodist Episcopal Church in 1902. His two most famous hymns are "Stand By Me" and "We'll Understand It Better By and By." It's said that when Thomas Dorsey first heard Tindley's spiritual called "I Do, Don't You," he quit writing popular music and turned to gospel songs.

Another composer of gospel hymns, Harry Thacker Burleigh, was the first to take the spiritual to the concert stage. Born in Erie, Pennsylvania, in 1866, Burleigh earned a scholarship to the National Conservatory of Music in New York City, where he often visited the home of its director, Czech composer Antonin Dvorak. After graduation, Burleigh became a concert artist, composer, arranger, and singer, traveling throughout the United States and Europe. In all, he composed some 100 songs, but he is best known for his solo arrangements of spirituals, especially "Deep River" and "Nobody Knows the Trouble I've Seen."

Before Burleigh, spirituals were performed mainly by choral groups, but his arrangements allowed some of the great musical voices of the time to sing them. And through these performances, heard over and again through the decades, more and more Americans came to appreciate the quality and value of these unique musical compositions.

SOMETHING TO PLEASE [E]

IS EVER A WATCHWORD WITH THE MANAGE[R]

BAIRD'S MAMMOTH M[

Which is now Absolutely The Strongest Show!   The Greatest Show!   The Best Show [

THE BEST

PLENTY OF

THE BEST

AND

NOTHING BUT

THE BEST

IS THE

SECRET

OF OUR

SUBLIME

SUCCESS.

PROMINENT IN THE ATTRACTIVE PRO[C]

THE GRAND IDEAL CLOG BALL[

6

The Minstrel Show

The things that you're liable to read in the Bible,
It ain't necessarily so.

AFTER THE CIVIL War, black Americans well understood the lyrics to George Gershwin's famous song from *Porgy and Bess*. The Union had triumphed, slavery was outlawed, all people were free. Well, it wasn't necessarily so. During Reconstruction, an attempt was made to rebuild the South and its economy after the devastation of the war. Well intentioned as it might have been, it was filled with corruption, greed, and turmoil. And even with the aid of such agencies as the Freedmen's Bureau, many of the ex-slaves found themselves right back on the plantations—free, perhaps, but working as hard as before, and for the same masters. What else could they do? The "forty acres and a mule" promised to them by the government never seemed to materialize.

Once again, music stepped in to soothe troubled spirits. As blacks moved from work on the farms and plantations to work in the cities, in the factories,

A newspaper ad promotes an upcoming minstrel performance. Following the Civil War, many talented black musicians performed in traveling minstrel shows, but minstrel performances originated with white performers portraying stereotypes of black society.

and on the railroads, they took their music with them—from "Michael, Row the Boat Ashore" to John Henry's ever-present story of a "steel driving man." These railroad songs, as they were known, never lost their popularity. Neither did the influence of the black church on gospel music. The fact that trouble did not end with freedom was repeated in the words of many songs. And the suffering was expressed in many ways:

> Sometimes I feel like a motherless child
> A long ways from home.

After the Civil War, the minstrel show, an old musical form that began about 1830 and enjoyed a golden age until the start of the war—gained in popularity once again. This form of entertainment was the first truly American contribution to the theater, and it owed everything to the music and mannerisms of black people, mainly slaves. However, at first it was not performed by black people.

The first minstrels were white men with blackened faces. They darkened their skin with burnt cork and imitated the songs, dances, and speech patterns of black Americans on the plantations. Although initially not intended to be cruel, these performances by white minstrels became increasingly so during and after the Civil War. The resulting stereotypes of black people as stupid and shiftless, or outlandish in manner and dress, helped to keep alive the bigotry that unfortunately was rooted in American society.

The first group minstrel show was performed by white men in blackface in New York City in 1843. Called the Virginia Minstrels, they were led by one of the outstanding composers of minstrel songs, Daniel Decatur Emmett (1815–1904), a white man.

Emmett was born in Ohio, the son of a blacksmith. He joined the army at the age of 18. After his

White minstrels, seen here in their typical "blackface" for performance, helped to develop many stereotypes of black society. Although not originally intended to be cruel, many minstrel shows helped promote bigotry toward African Americans during the 1800s.

discharge, he played the drum in traveling circus bands. He was also accomplished on the flute and violin. After leaving the Virginia Minstrels, Emmett joined Bryant's Minstrels, and in 1859 he wrote a song called "Dixie." It later became the unofficial song of the Confederacy during the Civil War and today is still a designation for the South. The name supposedly came from the dividing line between North and South, the Mason-Dixon line. However, there is some dispute over this. A correspondent for Boston's *Evening Transcript* said that he had heard the song before Emmett published it, and that it came from New Orleans and had its origins in black music. Supposedly, the word *dixie* came not from Mason-Dixon

Daniel Decatur Emmett is one of the more widely remembered composers of minstrel songs. His most famous song, "Dixie," was written in 1859.

but from the French word *dix*, meaning "ten." The word appeared on $10 bills from Louisiana, which before 1860 were printed in both English and French.

The typical minstrel performance had two parts, or acts. The first part included comic routines, some ballads of the day, a closing song by all members of the troupe, and a walkaround. During the latter, each performer walked around the inside of the semicircle formed by the rest of the troupe and then offered his specialty—song, dance, or musical instrument—from the center of the stage. The second part was known as the olio, or miscellaneous collection, in this case of musical selections. It usually included female impersonations (since all the members of the troupe were male), various specialty dances and acts, and a burlesque, or spoof, of some current popular drama. The music for the minstrel show came from the banjo, violin, tambourine, and other drumlike instruments.

One of the most popular of the white minstrels was Thomas Dartmouth Rice, a performer known as Daddy. Rice based his entire routine on the songs and dances he had seen performed by an elderly crippled black man named Jim Crow. Supposedly, the old man sang as he went about his work cleaning the stables. His deformed leg produced a shuffle as he walked, punctuated by a periodic jump into the air at different points in his song. This kind of shuffling dance was known as the Jim Crow—actually the "Jump Jim Crow"—routine. Its ridiculing nature was handed down through the decades, and the name was eventually used to designate the infamous Jim Crow segregation laws in the U.S. South.

America's greatest white composer of minstrel tunes was Stephen Foster (1826–1864). His songs stem directly from the black music he heard as a child, when he regularly attended church with one of the family servants. As an adult, he began writing "Ethiopian" songs—the term used for black music by whites, who supposedly surmised that all slaves came from that far-off country in eastern Africa. Foster's most lasting contributions to minstrel music were "Old Folks at Home," "Camptown Races," "Old Black Joe," My Old Kentucky Home," and "Massa's in de Cold, Cold Ground." A group called the Christy Minstrels featured many of his songs. In the 20th century, the New Christy Minstrels delighted audiences once again.

Often compared with Stephen Foster but far less well known was James Bland, whose sentimental

This magazine story shows an example of the Jim Crow character portrayed by Thomas Dartmouth Rice, a white man, during his minstrel performances.

138   HARPER'S NEW MONTHLY MAGAZINE.

T. D. RICE AS THE ORIGINAL "JIM CROW."
From the collection of Thomas J. McKee, Esq.

queer hat, very much pointed down before and behind, and very much cocked on one side." He went to England in 1836, where he met with great success, laid the foundation of a very comfortable fortune, and personally and professionally he was the Buffalo Bill of the London of half a century ago. Mr. Ireland, speaking of his popularity in this country, says that he drew more money to the Bowery Theatre than any other performer in the same period of time.

Rice was the author of many of his own farces, notably *Bone Squash* and *The Virginia Mummy*, and he was the veritable originator of the *genus* known to the stage as the "dandy darky," represented particularly in his creations of "Dandy Jim of Caroline" and "Spruce Pink." He died in 1860, never having forfeited the respect of the public or the good-will of his fellow-men.

There were many lithographed and a few engraved portraits of Rice made during the years of his great popularity, a number of which are still preserved. In

Other cities besides Louisville claim Jim Crow. Francis Courteney Wemyss, in his *Autobiography*, says he was a native of Pittsburgh, whose name was Jim Cuff; while Mr. Robert P. Nevin, in the *Atlantic Monthly* for November, 1867, declares that the original was a negro stage-driver of Cincinnati, and that Pittsburgh was the scene of Rice's first appearance in the part, a local negro there, whose professional career was confined to holding his mouth open for pennies thrown to him on the docks and the streets, furnishing the wardrobe for the initial performance.

Rice was born in the Seventh Ward of New York in 1808. He was a supernumerary at the Park Theatre, where "Sam" Cowell remembered him in *Bombastes Furioso*, attracting so much attention by his eccentricities that Hilson and Barnes, the leading characters in the cast, made a formal complaint, and had him dismissed from the company, Cowell adding that this man, whose name did not even appear in the bills, was the only actor on the stage whom the audience seemed to notice. Cowell also describes him in Cincinnati in 1829 as a very unassuming, modest young man, who wore "a very

JAMES ROBERTS IN THE SONG "MASSA GEORGE WASHINGTON AND MASSA LAFAYETTE."
From the collection of Thomas J. McKee, Esq.

songs also glorified the Old South. He was born in New York City in 1854 to middle-class, mixed white, black, and Indian parents. Bland first heard banjo music on the streets of Philadelphia, where the family moved when he was six. He saved enough money to buy a banjo and taught himself to play.

By the time Bland finished high school, the family had moved to Washington, D.C., and he entered the all-black Howard University. Although headed for law school, his heart was elsewhere, so he dropped out and pursued a musical career. In 1875, he joined the Original Black Diamonds, a minstrel group based in Boston. Five years later he became one of Haverly's Genuine Colored Minstrels, black men who nonetheless performed in blackface. The troupe performed in London in 1881 and made a hit with Bland's own composition "O Dem Golden Slippers."

Bland did not return to the United States until the early 1900s, eventually settling once again in Philadelphia. But minstrel shows were on the way out, and Bland's music was no longer in vogue. He died penniless in 1911 at the age of 56. Although James Bland wrote more than 600 songs, probably his most well known is "Carry Me Back to Old Virginny," a song most people think was composed by Stephen Foster. But Bland wrote it when he was 24 years old. Since 1940, it has been Virginia's state song.

After the Civil War, more and more black performers got into the world of minstrelsy—one of the few places where a black entertainer could get along in the white world. Although there had been some groups performing earlier, the first successful black group, the Brooker and Clayton Georgia Minstrels, was organized about 1865. They billed themselves as "The Only Simon Pure Negro Troupe in the World." They were 21 highly talented musicians who probably could have found better work elsewhere had their skin been a different color. However, they were much admired in the United States and called the "masters of minstrelsy." P. T. Barnum, the renowned circus showman, said they were "extraordinary and the best I ever saw." They toured Europe in 1877 and sang for Queen Victoria of England in 1883. The largest known black minstrel company was Calender's Consolidated Spectacular

A magazine advertisement heralds the arrival of Primrose and West's Big Minstrels. Although many minstrel performances portrayed blacks in stereotypical fashion, some African-American musicians and performers found that minstrel shows were one route to acceptance in white society.

Colored Minstrels, organized in 1882. Black entertainers still had a long way to go before they would be accepted purely on the basis of their talent, but the minstrel show did help to pave the way.

Toward the end of the 19th century, the popularity of minstrelsy began to fade. White entertainers in the North were developing shows in a more colorful and elegant style, which would eventually become the musical comedy. Some of the early black minstrel acts were eventually absorbed into vaudeville, a new form taking hold in the 1880s. This light entertainment, consisting of some dozen unrelated acts featuring singers, dancers, comedians, jugglers, and much else, would last until the 1930s.

Interestingly, even though black entertainers began to be featured in vaudeville, so did the white man in blackface. Probably the most popular was Al Jolson (1886–1950), a singer and comedian who in 1918, his face blackened, transformed an unsuccessful Gershwin song called "Swanee" into his trademark. Jolson also made film history when in 1927 he starred in the first talking motion picture, *The Jazz Singer*.

Al Jolson, who became famous for his performances in black-face and is seen here applying his makeup, appeared in the first talking motion picture.

7

From Ragtime and the Blues to Jazz

Let me see you do the rag-time dance.

Gonna git myself a rowboat
    and head for the other side;
Oh what I'd give to hear
    those Memphis Blues once more.

GOSPEL EVOLVED INTO many forms in its travels throughout many years. One of the first was ragtime—a kind of music intended for the black musician alone, an expression of individuality. Of course, in time it was picked up into so-called white music as well. It's said that the name might have come from the colorful bandannas, or squares of cotton, that slaves wore around the neck and head while working in the hot fields.

Sounding very different from the usual style of piano music from Europe, ragtime, or piano-rag, music was played in "ragged" time, a musical form in which the right hand plays the melody while the left hand makes "stomping" sounds on the keys. These variations may have been associated with black dancers using their heels as drums as well as the call-and-response form of the old slave work songs.

No one knows when rag first began. It may have originated with itinerant piano players along the Mississippi in the late 19th century. Music wasn't

Billie Holiday, one of the most influential blues singers of her time, in performance. The blues, ragtime, and jazz can all trace their origins back to gospel music.

written down at that time. However, the lone piano player in a river saloon was expected to simulate an entire orchestra for the patrons' listening or dancing pleasure. Rag may have been a way of providing more music from one player.

Many music historians mark the beginning of ragtime in 1892, when "Michigan Waters" was published by a black New Orleans pianist named Tony Jackson. In 1893, the word first appeared in sheet music with "Ma Ragtime Baby." Rag was even represented at the World's Columbian Exposition in Chicago that year. In 1897, Thomas Turpin, a pianist from St. Louis, Missouri, published "Harlem Rag." This self-taught musician, who stood more than six feet tall and weighed about 300 pounds, wrote many ragtime tunes, including "Rag-Time Nightmare" and "St. Louis Rag."

One of the many black musicians performing at the Chicago fair in 1893 was a 25-year-old piano player from Texarkana, Texas, named Scott Joplin, the man who would one day be crowned King of Ragtime. Joplin was born into a musical family: his mother played the banjo, his father played the violin, one brother played both instruments, and the other brother sang. But young Scott had special talent for the piano, and he began to take lessons from local black musicians. In his early teens, Joplin began playing up and down the Mississippi Valley. Influenced by older musicians around him, he picked up the peculiar style of ragtime and decided he liked it.

Joplin left the 1893 fair in Chicago with a feeling that black music was beginning to be respected. That was more important to him than his own success. He wanted ragtime to gain the place that classical music held in the minds and hearts of most audiences.

Joplin enrolled at Smith College of Music in Sedalia, Missouri, for more training. In 1899, he pub-

Scott Joplin, considered the King of Ragtime, was one of the first black performers to have his works published. Joplin's success helped other African-American performers win exposure to a wider audience.

lished "Maple Leaf Rag," now a classic. It became a landmark in the history of American music and was a financial success for Joplin.

Scott Joplin became very popular in the early years of the 20th century. But his desire to see ragtime elevated to the status of classical music had become an obsession. In 1903, he composed his first so-called ragtime opera, *A Guest of Honor*. It was never published as a complete work and the manuscript has since been lost. In 1911, Joplin finished his second opera. Called *Treemonisha*, the work was not ragtime but a serious effort to create a classic that would compare with the best in European music. It was a tremendous undertaking. The piano version, which Joplin published at his own expense, totaled 230 pages, and the three-act opera used 11 soloists. But the King of Ragtime could find no one to

The cover of Scott Joplin's sheet music for "Maple Leaf Rag."

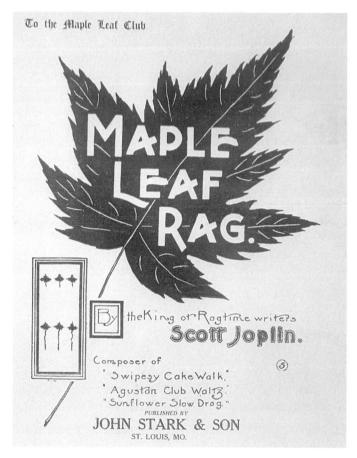

produce his work. So, with the help of a friend, he organized a single performance, in Harlem, performed without scenery, costumes, or an orchestra. The audience disapproved, and Joplin never recovered from the disappointment. Given to increasing periods of dark depression, Scott Joplin died in New York City in 1917. He was 49 years old.

Joplin never lived to see his dream come true, but he probably would have been pleased with the revival of his music in the 1970s. It was partially sparked by the award-winning film *The Sting* (1973), in which Paul Newman and Robert Redford play two small-time con men from Chicago who successfully outwit a high roller from New York City. Joplin's ragtime music, arranged by Oscar-winning Marvin

Ragtime piano player Eubie Blake performs with Noble Sissle in 1926. The popularity of ragtime continues to this day.

Hamlisch, runs throughout the film. Two years later, Joplin's beloved *Treemonisha* was produced in Houston, Texas, and eventually played on Broadway.

In the early years of the 20th century, a commercialized style of rag became popular in New York City, the center of the music publishing business. It was written and played mostly by white musicians who had learned it from their black counterparts. This type of piano playing produced a "tinny" sound that gave the school of ragtime its name—Tin Pan Alley. New York's music publishing world is still known by that name. And ragtime continues to delight modern-day audiences. At the turn of the 21st century, a musical entitled *Tin Pan Alley Rag* was playing to audiences on Broadway.

Ragtime wasn't the only music to come from gospel. Around the turn of the 20th century, a

Blues singer Ma Rainey, seen here performing with her Georgia Blues Band, developed a popular style often referred to as city or classic blues.

different sound was drifting out of the Mississippi Valley and out of Tin Pan Alley. It would overtake rag in popularity and endurance. Whether played or sung by black or white performers, it was associated with the haunting heartaches of life and thus came to be called the blues.

The blues originated from "sorrow songs," which dealt with, for example, laments from slaves or the despair of poor blacks without jobs and with a bleak future. The songs were the cries of people who had nothing and expected nothing. The blues singers would wail about losing jobs, homes, and friends, but most of all, about losing sweethearts. "St. Louis Blues," written by W. C. Handy in 1914, captured the essence of the blues:

> I hate to see de evening sun go down,
> Hate to see de evening sun go down, . . .
> Cause my baby he done left dis town.

Not all blues songs were sad, however. In some, there was a good deal of sly optimism. Lost your job? Well, hop on a train tomorrow morning and find a new one. Lost your girl (guy)? Somebody better looking may be at the next station, too. Or, how about this little comment on life's tough situations?

I've got the blues, but I'm too darn mean to cry,
I've got the blues, but I'm too darn mean to cry,
Before I'd cry, I'd rather lay down and die.

Or, on the difference between the sexes:

When a woman gets the blues she hangs her head and
    cries,
When a woman gets the blues she hangs her head and
    cries,
But when a man gets the blues, he grabs a train and
    flies.

Some music historians separate the blues into three phases. The first phase was known as country blues, popular in the Mississippi Delta area. It used a guitar without modern amplification and was often sung with a rough voice for emphasis. The second phase—city or classic blues, which lasted from about the 1920s to the 1930s—was mainly dominated by female singers such as Ma Rainey and Bessie Smith. The songs had regular beginnings and endings and the singer was usually accompanied by two or more instruments. The third phase—called contemporary blues—was B. B. King's type of music, with electric guitars and saxophones and a kind of louder quality to the singing voice.

William Christopher Handy, the man most associated with the blues, did not start this style of music. No one knows who did. The earliest known professional blues singer, Ma Rainey, said she first heard a blues song in 1902. Born in Columbus, Georgia, as Gertrude Pridgett, she was singing in traveling shows at an early age. When she married Will Rainey, a dancer and comedian better known as Pa, it seemed natural that she would be called Ma. Her touring career lasted some 30 years. When she began singing sorrowful tunes in her act, the audiences loved them.

W. C. Handy, seen here having a laugh with Nat King Cole, has been called the Father of the Blues. Cole would later portray Handy in the film St. Louis Blues.

According to Rainey, they kept asking her what she was singing, and she finally said, "It's the blues." However, other old-timers disagree, claiming that the blues was just always the blues. When Baltimore's Eubie Blake, famous for his eastern school of rag music, was asked about blues in Baltimore, he answered, "Why, Baltimore *is* the blues!"

Handy may not have started the blues, but he certainly made the blues popular. When he heard a man singing a song in a Mississippi train station in 1903, he recognized the sad sound as something different. And he set out to give that sound to the music-loving public.

W. C. Handy was born in 1873 in Florence, Alabama. He grew up loving all kinds of music, perhaps because both his father and grandfather were Methodist ministers. He organized a quartet to play in the Chicago Exposition in 1893, but that soon disbanded. Performing over the next several years with a minstrel group, he played everything from classical to Irish ballads. But after he heard the sad singing in the Mississippi train station, he decided to return to the type of music sung in the old slave fields of the South.

Handy actually went out on a lone search to find the blues. In river saloons and along the docks, he listened to the songs of the workers. Then he went home and composed. His first published work was "Memphis Blues" (1912). It spoke of the sorrow of one's lot in life and was tremendously popular.

> The Mississippi river is long, deep and wide
> Gonna git myself a rowboat and head for other side.
> Oh what I'd give to hear those Memphis blues once
>   more.

Unfortunately for Handy, he gained little money from its success. He had published "Memphis Blues" himself, and when a Memphis promoter offered $100 for the rights to the song, Handy agreed. He needed the money. When the words were later added and the song published in New York, he received no royalties.

The Father of the Blues never made much money from his efforts until his later years, when various anthologies of his work were released and his autobiography, *Father of the Blues,* was published in 1941. His life came to the silver screen in 1958, the year of his death, with the highly fictionalized *St. Louis Blues,* which starred the great balladeer Nat King Cole as the great Handy.

If you listen to a blues song, you can often sense the fuzzy line that separates it from an old spiritual. The words from a spiritual

> Going to the graveyard
> To lay this body down

become

> Don't count your chickens
> Chickens you can keep
> Chickens come high but the blues come cheap
> So bow your head and bend it low
> And play the funeral blues.

This mixing of the old spirituals and the blues is kept alive today in funeral processions, especially in

New Orleans. They are impressive parades, with a flower-draped coffin and gaily dressed marchers slow-stepping through the streets of the city to the wail of mournful trumpets:

> You can hear the brass today sounding out
> Lord, I want to be in that number
> When the saints go marching in.

Interestingly, another black music form, now almost totally extinct, is also given some credit for bringing on the blues. It was known as cries, calls, and hollers, a musical tradition among rural blacks in the South. Like the song that W. C. Handy heard in the Mississippi train station, this was the music that sustained workers during the days of slavery.

It seems almost impossible to distinguish a cry, or a call, from a holler, and in fact some of the names just seemed to depend on location. Some areas might have said a "cottonfield holler," others a "cornfield cry." They all did the same thing: they allowed the field workers to keep contact with each other as they toiled in the hot fields. One worker would start singing, another would sing a response, still another would reply until perhaps the whole field was alive with song. Even though these types of calls lent themselves to field work, city peddlers had their own forms of such music, too, even in the North.

One of the most famous of all early blues singers was Bessie Smith (1898–1937), "the Empress of the Blues." Born to a poor family in Chattanooga, Tennessee, she was helped into the musical world by Ma Rainey. After touring saloons and theaters in the South, she made her first recording, for Columbia, in 1923. A confident artist and beautiful woman, she was a commanding presence on stage, singing of poverty, lost love, and cruelty. A short motion picture, *St. Louis Blues* (1929), tells of her strife but was

Bessie Smith, "the Empress of the Blues," was one of the most famous of the early blues performers. A film that depicts parts of her life can be seen today at the Museum of Modern Art in New York City.

banned because it was "too real." Today, it is preserved in the Museum of Modern Art in New York City. In 1937, Bessie Smith died of injuries from an automobile accident. The charge was made by some that had she been white, she would have received earlier medical treatment and might have survived. Playwright Edward Albee wrote of this in his play *The Death of Bessie Smith* (1960). Her biography, by Chris Albertson, was published in 1972.

The blues live on through the music of W. C. Handy, Ma Rainey, Bessie Smith, and a host of more modern performers, such as Billie Holiday, Jelly Roll Morton, Dinah Washington, and B. B. King.

Yet another musical form grew out of the musical traditions of gospel, ragtime, and the blues: the uniquely American style called jazz. It's difficult to describe jazz without hearing it and just as hard to pinpoint its history. Dr. Alain Locke, who wrote about black music in the 1930s, said that from black folk music came the melody and rhythm that is ragtime, and that carried over to orchestration and harmony, which is jazz.

Others say that jazz is part of a continuum of black music—from gospel and spirituals to ragtime, to the blues, to jazz.

No one knows exactly when jazz began, but most authorities agree that it was probably in the early 20th century and that it came out of the same areas as ragtime and the blues. That meant towns in the Mississippi Valley and, of course, the city of New Orleans. In fact, one of the most distinct styles of jazz is called New Orleans jazz. And because this city developed like no other in the United States, this type of jazz could only have flourished there.

During its precolonial history of occupation by France and Spain, New Orleans became home to three racial groups—whites, blacks, and Creoles, people of mixed black and French or Spanish ancestry. Although all three groups lived fairly separate lives, they got along reasonably well, until after the Civil War. As many newly freed blacks entered the city, New Orleans began to pass some restrictive codes. The result was the forced merging of blacks and Creoles into living and working areas. In time, both racial groups began to listen to each other's music. Where ragtime had depended upon the piano, a new sound developed that used many instruments—piano, drums, brasses, banjos—to provide the rhythm. With more instruments, there was more opportunity for making up—or improvising—new sounds on the spot. And out of this came New Orleans jazz.

Jelly Roll Morton sits at his piano. One of the first true jazz composers, Morton would help put New Orleans jazz on the map.

Probably the greatest name in early New Orleans jazz is that of Ferdinand La Menthe, better known as Jelly Roll Morton. He was probably the first genuine jazz composer. A Creole born in New Orleans around 1885, he learned music from his carpenter/trombonist father and composed his first tune, "New Orleans Blues," at the age of 17. Morton is said to have bridged the gap between ragtime and jazz piano styles. His playing was lighter, more swinging than rag. By the time he was 19, Morton was on the move, playing and composing as he went. His famous "King Porter Stomp," written in Mobile, Alabama, in the early years of the 20th century, was used as a theme song for many years by famed bandleader Benny Goodman.

Morton was the first to write down a jazz arrangement. His "Jelly Roll Blues," written in Chicago in 1915, was probably the first such publication. But he wrote many classics as well and became the toast of Chicago, New York, and the entire country. From 1926 until 1928, Morton and his Red Hot Peppers recorded a number of compositions for Victor records. Critics cite these as evidence of Jelly Roll Morton's jazz genius. In 1940, Morton moved to Los Angeles following the death of his grandmother. He died there the following year, at the age of 56.

Jazz evolved into other styles as well, the best known probably being swing, which was dominated from the 1920s to the 1940s mainly by white bands—Benny Goodman, Artie Shaw, and Tommy Dorsey, to name a few. But the influence of black musicians was felt here as well, most notably by two great names in the field of music and jazz, Louis Armstrong and Duke Ellington.

Louis Armstrong was born in 1900 in New Orleans. He was to become perhaps the most influential name in all of jazz. By the time of his death in 1971, Satchmo—as he was affectionately called by his adoring fans—was known worldwide, not only for his trumpet but for his toothy grin and scat singing, a singing style that uses the voice as a musical instrument, substituting nonsense syllables for the words. One of the all-time greats, Ella Fitzgerald, who sometimes recorded with Armstrong, also made scat singing her own trademark.

When it came to cool, sophisticated jazz, there was none better or greater than Edward Kennedy "Duke" Ellington. Born in Washington, D.C., in 1899, Ellington and his orchestra became the toast of New York City, especially at the famous Cotton Club. During his lifetime, Ellington composed more than 2,000 songs. Some of his most memorable melodies

were "Mood Indigo," "Sophisticated Lady," "Solitude," and "I Got It Bad and That Ain't Good." In 1969, he received the Presidential Medal of Freedom, this country's highest civilian honor. Duke Ellington died in 1974, his reputation secure as one of America's most outstanding musicians.

Duke Ellington became famous as the leader of the Cotton Club's jazz orchestra in New York City.

8

Modern Gospel in America

Deep in my heart, I do believe,
We shall overcome some day.

MODERN GOSPEL ENTERED the lives of all Americans in a new way in the 1950s. After years of quiet suffering and injustice for African Americans, perhaps it was fitting that the civil rights movement began in a quiet, almost unnoticed way, too. On December 1, 1955, Rosa Parks, a black seamstress in Montgomery, Alabama, refused to give up her seat on a bus to a white man, which was the custom. Blacks could sit in the back of the bus unless all the seats for whites were filled. When Parks refused to give up her seat, she was arrested. Thus began a 369-day boycott of Montgomery public transportation. When it was over, a new black leader—Rev. Martin Luther King Jr.—had emerged to shape a program of nonviolent resistance.

The Civil Rights Act of 1957, the first in about 75 years, was not considered enough. Both blacks and whites alike wanted more change. In subtle and important ways, they began to resist nonviolently:

A woman claps her hands and sings along with the other members of her gospel choir. Gospel continues to flourish in the United States and has influenced the vast majority of modern American music.

Johnny Cash is one of many country musicians who have incorporated gospel into their performances. Such Cash songs as "Ring of Fire" tap into many of the same qualities that originated with the very first gospel songs.

they sat in at previously all-white lunch counters; they marched through the streets of major cities and the nation's capital; they demanded fairness, freedom, and equal justice. And as they marched and protested, they sang an old spiritual that soon became the theme song of the entire movement and period:

> We shall overcome, we shall overcome
> We shall overcome some day
> For I know in my heart, it will come true
> We shall overcome some day.

Gospel has also become a solid part of another American musical form—country. Some speak of this merger of gospel and country as "hillbilly hymns," represented by songs such as "Just a Closer Walk with Thee" and "I Saw the Light," popularized by Hank Williams and Johnny Cash. This mixture of gospel with country enjoys great popularity today. Several organizations have sprung up to promote country/gospel, including the North America Country Music Association, which was formed in 1997.

The popularity of modern gospel might trace its roots back to 1940, when the Ward Singers became the first black vocal group to record a gospel song that sold more than one million copies. The hymn was "Surely God Is Able," written by W. Herbert Brewster, a Memphis Baptist minister. By 1981, James Cleveland, a minister, composer, arranger, and singer, became the first black gospel artist with a star on Hollywood's Walk of Fame. Today gospel music has become part of the mainstream entertainment business. It is listed as a category for the Grammy Awards, which honor the best in various musical fields. Since 1969, the Gospel Music Association has presented the Dove Awards for the best in gospel, with traditional and contemporary awards for white and black gospel artists.

An example of gospel in one of its most modern forms can be seen in a performance by Kirk Franklin, a gospel conductor-composer who combines hip-hop music with gospel—which sometimes drives gospel purists to distraction. At the beginning of a typical concert, Franklin tells his fans, "For those of you who came to hear church music, we have that here tonight. For those who came to hear hip-hop, we got that here tonight. And for all of you who want to get your praise on, you can do that tonight." After telling the crowd about his experience of being saved by Christ, he and his 17-member choir devote all their energy to a gospel tune such as "Something About the Name of Jesus." Then he gets the bleachers rocking with his band, which delivers some hip-hop and rap. In rare moments of rest, Franklin exhorts his fans to "stand up and hug their nearest neighbors." The audiences seem to love it.

Another gospel leader of what is said to be the "fastest growing church in America" is Bishop T. D. Jakes of the Potter's House congregation in Dallas, Texas. Born in Charleston, West Virginia, in 1957, Jakes says he grew up carrying a Bible and preaching to imaginary congregations. He delivers his message via cable television, books, the Internet, and of course spirituals. His powerful sermons are backed in impressive style by the 300-voice Potter's House Mass Choir. In 1998, Jakes received a Grammy nomination for a CD of his best-seller, *Woman, Thou Art Loosed!*, which features his own singing. In 1999, his gospel-pop album, *Live from the Potter's House*, was released.

In New York City, Lincoln Center Festival '99 celebrated gospel music with a choir drawn from more than 20 churches and groups, and songs that ran from pop-funk gospel to the music of the purists. The performance included a 30-minute tribute to Thomas A. Dorsey, father of black gospel music. The evening reached its high point when Shirley Caesar, one of gospel's greatest modern figures, sang Dorsey's "Take My Hand, Precious Lord."

Another concert held in 1999 at Lincoln Center celebrated the three so-called Sacred Concerts of Duke Ellington. When first performed in 1965, 1968, and 1973, Ellington insisted that they were not "jazz masses," but instead "people talking to people about God." This complicated concert took the best of all three works and condensed it into two and a half hours. Once again, Shirley Caesar was featured.

Despite all his success in popular music, Ellington once claimed that the Sacred Concerts were "the most important thing I've ever done or am ever

James Cleveland stands behind the other members of the James Cleveland Singers. Cleveland is the first black gospel performer to have his name honored with a star on Hollywood's Walk of Fame.

likely to do." One of them, *Black, Brown and Beige*, is a multimovement work about the history of black people. One section, called "Come Sunday," tells about the worship practices of slaves before the Civil War: "Come Sunday, while all the whites had gone into the church, the slaves congregated under a tree. Huddled together, they passed the word of God around in whispers." "Come Sunday" has now become a jazz standard.

The close ties between gospel, blues, jazz, and popular music are reflected in the long list of black singing stars who came from religious music backgrounds and entered the world of popular music with relative ease. Here are just a few.

Sam Cooke was born in Clarksdale, Mississippi, in 1931. His father, a minister, moved the family of eight children to Chicago a few years later. When Cooke was 19, he began singing with a group called the Soul Stirrers, which included two of his sisters and one brother. But in 1956, when he recorded a pop tune called "Loveable," he used the name Dale Cooke on the label. He was afraid of upsetting the gospel group with whom he was also singing. However, Cooke's success with pop music soon became common knowledge, and he went on to a successful career, which included his multimillion-copy hit "You Send Me," a song he wrote with his brother, L. C. Cooke.

Sarah Vaughan, a singer with an extraordinary voice and range, became a legend in her own time. She was born into a musical family in Newark, New Jersey, in 1924. Her father played the guitar and sang folk songs; her mother played the piano and sang in a Baptist church choir, which Vaughan later joined—but not for long. In 1943 she won an amateur-night contest at New York's Apollo Theater. Vocalist Billy Eckstine was struck by her talent and recommended her for the Earl Hines Orchestra, with whom he was currently singing. Through the years, the timbre of her voice deepened, and her ability to use her voice

An appearance at an amateur-night contest at the Apollo Theater would propel Sarah Vaughan from virtual unknown to legend. The extraordinary range and power of her voice made her one of the most dynamic jazz performers of her time.

The first black artist to have his own radio and television shows, Nat King Cole was one of the most beloved performers of his time. His trademark style and grace continue to captivate music lovers to this day.

as a musical instrument was astonishing. In both the jazz and pop fields, her outstanding recordings include "Misty," "Tenderly," "Lullaby of Birdland," and perhaps her biggest commercial hit, "Broken Hearted Melody." A heavy smoker all her life, Sarah Vaughan died of lung cancer in 1990.

Remember that great singer called Ruth Jones? Probably not. Ruth Jones sang gospel in the Salle Martin choir in Chicago. But, like Mahalia Jackson, Jones believed that gospel and pop don't mix. So, when she decided to switch to popular music, she left gospel behind and changed her name to Dinah Washington. Although she grew up in Chicago, Washington was born in Tuscaloosa, Alabama, in 1924, and won an amateur contest at the age of 15. Her crystal-clear diction and penetrating, high-pitched voice made her a superstar in both the rhythm and blues and pop fields. She died at the age of 39 from an accidental overdose of diet pills and alcohol.

Another singer with early ties to the church was Nat King Cole, who was born in Montgomery, Alabama, in 1919 and raised in Chicago. His father was a minister and Nat sang in the church choir as a child. With his mother as his only piano teacher, he became an accomplished pianist by the age of 12 and formed his own band in high school. In 1946, he became the first black to have his own radio show; later he would become the first black to have his own TV show. From "Straighten Up and Fly Right" through "Mona Lisa" and "Nature Boy," Nat King Cole became one of the most beloved and prolific popular artists of his time. Another heavy smoker, he died of lung cancer in 1965.

Cole and his second wife, Maria Ellington (no relation to Duke Ellington), had a daughter in 1950, named Natalie Maria. She would grow up to be a top recording star in her own right. When Natalie began to record her father's songs—with the help of modern electronics, to sing with him—Nat Cole's career seemed to start all over again. Natalie Cole won a Grammy Award for her recording, combined with her father's voice, of his classic "Unforgettable."

The influence of gospel music is not confined to famous musicians, however. Individual people find ways to incorporate gospel into their fast-paced lives. One such person is Jane Sapp of Springfield, Massachusetts, a performer who uses gospel songs as she travels the world, getting people, especially children, to sing with her, to "build strong communities through story, song, and shared experience." In a special project in 1996, Sapp got children from around the country to come to the Berkshires in Massachusetts, where they recorded an album called *We've All Got Stories*, a combination of rap, boogie-woogie, and a "clamping, stomping spiritual." Today, she sits at the piano and draws the crowd in with a wave of her hand. Everybody gets the spirit when she hits her first notes:

> This little light of mine. I'm gonna let it shine
> Let it shine, let it shine, let it shine.

"Diversity," Sapp says, "is not a splash of color or merely an appreciation of other cultures. It is a profound transformation in our thinking about who and what processes contribute to the design of our society." When Sapp gets people to sing, she feels that the walls of prejudice and race come tumbling down. Music brings people together.

Like the good old gospel train, gospel music has kept rolling along, telling everyone to "Get on board, children, get on board." The music is alive and well. You can hear it at the Grand Old Opry in Nashville, Tennessee. You can hear it at a children's concert in a small town. It comes from boisterous crowds in Madison Square Garden or an elegant gathering at Lincoln Center in New York City. It's forever alive in the recordings of gospel great Mahalia Jackson and country star Johnny Cash. In concert halls and recording studios all across the country, the gospel train rolls on. And it can be found especially on any Sunday morning, when the church doors are open and the air rings with the sound of the strong, vibrant voices of the congregation and the choir singing their music.

CHRONOLOGY

August 1619	First slaves in British settlements in the New World land in Jamestown, Virginia.
1775–1783	Revolutionary War is fought; blacks in the service of both the Americans and the British are frequently assigned musical duties.
circa 1791	Newport Gardner becomes first African American to open a music school.
1793	The cotton gin is invented; by enabling cotton to be harvested more economically, the gin increases the need for slaves to work the South's cotton plantations.
1800s	Slaves combine Christian and Bible stories with traditional African rhythms to produce spirituals, a musical style that will form an important component of gospel music. Slaves working in the fields use music as a tool to communicate, for entertainment, and to express their tragic plight.
1861–1865	The Civil War, pitting the Northern states of the Union and the Southern states of the Confederacy, is fought. Thousands of blacks see action. Ultimately the Union triumphs and the institution of slavery is abolished.
October 6, 1871	The Fisk Jubilee Singers, an 11-person vocal ensemble made up entirely of blacks from former slave families, depart on a world tour to raise money for their school, Fisk University in Nashville, Tennessee. The hugely successful tour introduces spirituals to a worldwide audience.
1892	New Orleans pianist Tony Jackson publishes "Michigan Waters," which many music historians consider the beginning of ragtime.
1902	Charles A. Tindley, first recognized composer of gospel hymns, founds East Calvary Methodist Episcopal Church.

1920s	Thomas A. Dorsey, called "the Father of Gospel Music," writes more than 400 gospel songs influenced by jazz and the blues, setting the course for modern gospel music.
1934	Mahalia Jackson, "the Queen of the Gospel Song," makes her first recording, "God's Gonna Separate the Wheat from the Tare."
1940	The Ward Singers become the first black vocal group to sell one million copies of a song.
1946	Nat King Cole becomes the first black to have his own radio show; later he has his own TV show.
December 1, 1955	Rosa Parks ignites the civil rights movement by refusing to give up her bus seat to a white person. Gospel music plays a highly visible role in the struggle for civil rights.
1999	Lincoln Center celebrates the Sacred Concerts of Duke Ellington.

FURTHER READING

Brooks, Tilford. *America's Black Musical Heritage*. Englewood Cliffs, N.J.: Prentice-Hall, 1984.

De Lerma, Dominique-Rene. *Black Music in Our Culture*. Kent, Ohio: Kent State University Press, 1970.

_____. *Reflections on Afro-American Music*. Kent, Ohio: Kent State University Press, 1973.

Haskins, James. *Black Music in America*. New York: Crowell, 1987.

Johnson, James Weldon, and J. Rosamond Johnson. *The Books of American Negro Spirituals*. New York: Viking, 1953.

"The Original Do-Right Woman: Aretha Franklin," *Newsweek*, October 4, 1999.

Southern, Eileen. *The Music of Black Americans*. New York: Norton, 1971.

INDEX

INDEX

ROSE BLUE, an author and educator, has written more than 50 books, both fiction and nonfiction, for young readers. Her books have appeared as TV specials and have won many awards. A native New Yorker, she lives in the borough of Brooklyn.

CORINNE J. NADEN, a former U.S. Navy journalist and children's book editor, also has more than 50 books to her creidt. A freelance writer, she lives in Tarrytown, New York, where she shares living quarters with her two cats, Tigger and Tally Ho!

PICTURE CREDITS